HOW TO COOK HALLOUMI

vegetarian feasts
for every occasion

NANCY ANNE HARBORD

HOW TO COOK HALLOUMI

vegetarian feasts
for every occasion

NANCY ANNE HARBORD

A very special thanks to the multi-national cooks of Britain,
who have always inspired me.

✳

And thank you to Lee for letting me shoot this book in our very small
one-bedroom flat with only medium-level grumpiness.

Delicious from scratch
www.deliciousfromscratch.com

First published in Great Britain in 2016 by **Delicious from scratch**.
Albion Place,
Leeds
LS1 6JS

brunch

dinner

✳

✳

party!

✳

halloumi fries
with garlic mayonnaise 112

halloumi choux pastry fritters
with tomato and basil 116

habanero oil halloumi
with spelt za'atar crackers 120

spinach & halloumi pie
with filo pastry 124

battered halloumi & chips
with lemon pickled onions and coriander peas 130

roasted aubergine & halloumi pizza
with crème fraîche and nigella seed crust 136

spring greens & halloumi pizza
with fresh red chilli and oregano crust 140

broccoli & halloumi pizza
with pickled chillies and sumac crust 142

chewy, crunchy, nutty pizza dough
with a thin, crispy base and puffed, airy crust 146

halloumi & spinach tamales
with guacamole, chipotle cream and coriander salad 152

butternut squash & halloumi Wellington
with winter vegetables, Yorkshire pudding and garlic sauce 158

✳

vegetarians love halloumi

*

It is moist, chewy and tender. Salty, meaty and umami – all flavours and textures that are extremely welcome on a vegetarian plate.

But for too long, halloumi has been relegated to the realms of simple pan-frying. This cheese can do so much more.

Grated, cubed, layered and wrapped… Marinated, spiced and seasoned… Caramelised, roasted, baked and seared… Battered, braised, fried and melted… Get the very best out of halloumi cheese with these happy, healthy vegetarian recipes – each absolutely bursting with flavour.

This book presents a range of feasts – not just meals, but magnificent arrays, bright with fresh vegetables, spices and seasonings – each showing halloumi at its cheesiest, chewiest, saltiest best.

The recipes in this book are crowd-pleasers – dishes that will have diners fighting over the last scrap of delicious toasty cheese. Whether that's a lazy Sunday brunch, a quick weeknight dinner or an outstanding party spread that truly leaves your guests dazzled.

I am passionate about the joys of cooking and eating well. For me that means a diet rich in vegetables, whole grains, pulses and dairy, and making as much as humanly possible from scratch.

I have included easy guides in the book on how to make your own healthy pasta, bread, pastry and other doughs – I believe it is by making these kinds of things at home, from real ingredients, that we have some hope of balancing all that lovely, gooey cheese.

There are some ingredients in this book that may not be in everyone's store cupboard. I think these foods are special and might even be worth seeking out, but this doesn't mean they can't be easily substituted if you don't have them on hand – there are detailed instructions at the back of the book if needed.

Aside from the odd baking ingredient, almost nothing in this book is completely essential. These are casual recipes that can take a lot of variation and adaption. Enjoy!

*

It's time for halloumi to shine.

brunch

brunch

brunch

✳

whole wheat halloumi parathas
with garlic butter and fried egg 22

moist, creamy cornbread
with tomato, halloumi and green chilli 26

caramelised halloumi potato wedges
with sumac yoghurt 28

halloumi, watermelon & basil salad
with pomegranate, mint and tomato 32

halloumi 'bacon'
with smoky, meaty, salty, umami flavour 36

full English breakfast
with all the trimmings 38

halloumi bacon & mushroom sandwich
with Dijon mustard and crusty sourdough 42

croque madame
with halloumi bacon and fried egg 46

harissa halloumi salad
with tomato pesto and avocado 50

halloumi onion bhaji waffles
with poached egg and avocado 54

cheese toastie
with halloumi, Stilton and Gruyère 58

✳

For lazy weekends.

whole wheat halloumi parathas
with garlic butter and fried egg

✳

Learn how to make stuffed flatbreads and dazzle your friends and family. A quick, healthy dough woven with strands of halloumi and toasted quickly in a hot pan. Topped with a decadent brush of garlic butter and a runny fried egg.

serves 4

whole wheat halloumi parathas

300g/2 ⅓ cups whole grain spelt or atta flour
50g/½ stick butter, melted
½ pack halloumi, finely grated

Add the flour and 1 teaspoon flaky salt to a food processor and whizz to combine. Drizzle in the melted butter and blend to combine well. With the machine running, add enough boiling water (about 100g/7 tablespoons, it depends on your flour) to form a supple dough that is not sticky. Blend for 1-2 minutes to knead the dough, until it is smooth, soft and a little shiny. Cover in plastic wrap and rest for at least 10 minutes.

Divide the dough into 4 pieces – keep the dough balls covered in plastic wrap while you work. Roll 1 dough ball into a 20cm/8" round and sprinkle a quarter of the halloumi evenly over the dough round. Fold the edges of the dough in to completely cover the halloumi, making a rough hexagonal. Turn the package over, sprinkle with a little flour and roll out again into a 20cm/8" round.

Heat a large, heavy frying pan over medium heat until very hot (you don't need any extra oil). Add a stuffed paratha to the pan – it should bubble in about a minute and be spotted brown on the heated side. If it takes much longer than that, the paratha will dry out before it browns and become tough and inflexible, so adjust the heat accordingly. Flip the paratha after that first minute and cook for another minute to brown the other side. Keep the cooked parathas soft as you work by wrapping the stack in a clean, lightly damp tea towel.

garlic, lemon and herb butter

½ lemon, juice only
1 garlic clove, crushed
50g/½ stick butter
small handful fresh herbs

Juice the lemon, add the garlic to the lemon juice and set aside for 20 minutes – this effectively cooks the garlic. When the garlic is ready, melt the butter in a small saucepan, add the garlic (reserving about half the lemon juice) and cook on a very low heat for 5 minutes. Taste and season with a little flaky salt if needed, lots of pepper and more lemon juice if you fancy it a little more tart. Finely chop the herbs and stir into the butter, remove from the heat and set aside for serving.

fried eggs

4 eggs
truffle salt to sprinkle

Heat a little drizzle of oil over medium heat in a heavy frying pan until hot. Crack in the eggs, cover the pan and turn off the heat, leaving the eggs to steam for a few minutes, until the top layer of egg white is cooked. Sprinkle the yolks with a pinch of truffle salt.

✳

Brush the cooked parathas with garlic butter, sprinkle with a few herbs, top each one with a runny fried egg and serve.

moist, creamy cornbread
with tomato, halloumi and green chilli

✳

This cornbread is quick to make and bakes into a moist bread with a thick, golden crust. Studded with halloumi, corn, tangy tomatoes and chilli, it is unbelievably moreish.

serves 4/makes one loaf

40g/10 dried tomato halves
160g/1 cup polenta
160g/1 ⅓ cups plain flour
1 tablespoon baking powder
½ teaspoon baking soda
½ pack halloumi, finely grated
3-4 hot fresh green chillies, thinly sliced
1 corn on the cob, kernels removed
300ml/1 ¼ cups milk
2 tablespoons apple cider vinegar
1 tablespoon honey
2 tablespoons soy sauce
100ml/7 tablespoons cold-pressed rapeseed oil

Preheat the oven to 180°C/350°F. Cover the dried tomatoes with boiling water, leave to soften for about 20 minutes then finely chop. Grease a 23cm/9" loaf tin and dust with polenta. In a large bowl, whisk together the dry ingredients so everything is evenly combined. Stir through the tomato pieces, grated halloumi, chilli and corn. Mix in the milk, vinegar, honey, soy sauce and oil. Scrape the wet dough into the tin. Bake for 40-50 minutes until the top is very golden, the sides pull away from the edge of the pan and a toothpick comes out clean when inserted into the centre. This bread is very moist, so it can stay in the oven for quite a time, developing a thick, crisp crust. Leave to cool completely in the pan.

✳

Serve toasted with lashings of butter.

caramelised halloumi potato wedges
with sumac yoghurt

✻

Make healthy potato wedges dramatically better with a crispy halloumi coating, roasted until caramelised. Dip in thick, cooling yoghurt seasoned with tangy sumac, fresh lemon and garlic.

serves 4

halloumi potato wedges

800g/4 large potatoes
1 level tablespoon cornflour
¼ pack halloumi, finely grated

Preheat the oven to 200°C/400°F. Cut the potatoes into wedges and toss with the cornflour and a good drizzle of oil until evenly coated. Roast for 25 minutes, until the potatoes are lightly browned and just tender when poked with a knife.

Take the wedges out of the oven and carefully toss with the grated halloumi. Return to the oven for a further 10 minutes, stirring halfway through, until the cheese is evenly caramelised and very crispy. Season with a tiny bit of flaky salt and plenty of pepper.

sumac yoghurt

250g/8oz Greek yoghurt
1 teaspoon sumac
½ garlic clove, crushed
squeeze of lemon juice

Mix all the ingredients and season with ¼ teaspoon flaky salt.

✳

Dip the hot, crispy, cheesy wedges in the tart, lemony yoghurt, scraping up any caramelised halloumi bits that try to escape.

halloumi, watermelon & basil salad
with pomegranate, mint and tomato

✷

Hot, toasted halloumi crusted in earthy, nutty nigella seeds – layered on sweet, fruity watermelon and herby salad with garlic, lemon and chilli. Bright with pink pomegranate seeds and absolutely packed with healthy summer flavour.

serves 4

halloumi and watermelon salad

450g/1lb cherry tomatoes
½ cucumber
¼ medium watermelon
1 pomegranate
½ head romaine lettuce
handful mint, leaves only
handful basil, leaves only
1 pack halloumi
2 tablespoons nigella seeds

Cut the cherry tomatoes in half, thinly slice the cucumber, cut the watermelon into large cubes, deseed the pomegranate and separate the romaine leaves. Arrange the fruit and vegetables on the plates, scatter over the herbs and drizzle over the dressing. Set aside while you cook the halloumi.

Cut the halloumi into 2cm/1" cubes and pat dry with paper towel. Sprinkle the nigella seeds on a plate and press the halloumi cubes in the seeds on all sides – you won't get a complete coating, but some of them should stick. Heat a little drizzle of oil (just enough to stop the nigella seeds sticking) over medium heat in a heavy frying pan until hot. Add the halloumi and cook on all sides, turning carefully, until nicely browned.

lemon-garlic dressing

1 lemon, juice only
1 garlic clove, crushed
1-2 hot green chillies, thinly sliced
2 tablespoons cold-pressed oil

Juice the lemon, add the garlic to the lemon juice and set aside for 20 minutes – this effectively cooks the garlic. When the garlic is ready, stir through the chillies, season with a big pinch of flaky salt and whisk in the oil.

✳

Sprinkle the hot, nutty halloumi over the salad, toss with the lemon dressing and serve immediately.

halloumi 'bacon'

with smoky, meaty, salty, umami flavour

✳

This recipe is very simple, but there's something about it that can make you animalistic. Seasoned with smoked paprika and the powdered umami that is nutritional yeast, its savoury flavours enhance everything it touches.

makes 4 portions

½ pack halloumi, thinly sliced
2 teaspoons nutritional yeast
2 teaspoons smoked paprika
3 tablespoons cold-pressed rapeseed oil or <u>habanero oil (page 121)</u>

Mix the nutritional yeast and paprika with the oil on a flat plate. Coat the halloumi slices and marinate for 20 minutes.

When you're ready to serve, heat a heavy frying pan over medium heat until hot and fry the slices until lightly browned on both sides.

Return to the marinade-covered plate, rub over the remaining seasoning and serve immediately.

✳

Use halloumi bacon wherever you need a little smoky, savoury flavour. So everywhere.

full English breakfast
with all the trimmings

✱

The peak of British hangover cuisine – my version with smoky, marinated halloumi bacon, fried potato, roasted tomatoes, garlic mushrooms, creamy scrambled eggs, fresh avocado and sourdough toast. Yes. For lazy weekends with those you love.

serves 4

roasted tomatoes with sherry vinegar

300g/10oz cherry tomatoes
2 tablespoons sherry vinegar
1 teaspoon dried oregano

Heat the oven to 150°C/300°F. Slice the tomatoes in half and lay on a baking tray, cut side up. Dab a a little vinegar onto each tomato half and sprinkle over the oregano. Roast for about an hour until dried out, but still a little moist. Season with a little flaky salt and plenty of pepper.

fried slivers of potato

400g/2 large potatoes
few leaves of rosemary, sage or thyme

Slice the potatoes in 2mm/⅛" thin rounds, then stack the slices and cut into 1.5cm/½" diamond shapes. Heat a good drizzle of oil over medium heat in a heavy frying pan until hot. Sprinkle the potatoes in an even layer and leave to cook undisturbed until a crust has formed on that layer (a few minutes), then stir and repeat. When everything is nicely browned, chop the herbs and sprinkle over with ¼ teaspoon flaky salt and plenty of pepper.

big, fat, juicy garlic mushrooms

25g/¼ stick butter
1 garlic clove
4 large, flat mushrooms

Raise the oven to 200°C/400°F. Mix together the butter and garlic and season with a big pinch of flaky salt if using unsalted butter. Arrange the mushrooms, gills down, on a baking tray and roast for 10 minutes to remove some water. Take out of the oven, spread over the butter and roast for a further 10 minutes.

creamy, slow-scrambled eggs

8 eggs
2 tablespoons double cream

Beat the eggs to combine and season with ½ teaspoon flaky salt. Heat a little butter or oil in a medium saucepan over medium heat and cook, stirring frequently, until very creamy and just cooked. Drizzle over the cream.

to serve

1 recipe <u>halloumi bacon (page 36)</u>
4 slices sourdough toast, well buttered
1-2 ripe avocados
leftover chana masala (if you have it!)

If you're worried about timing, everything except the eggs can be kept warm in a low oven. When everything is ready, toast the bread, slice and season the avocado with a little flaky salt, reheat the chana masala (if using) and serve.

*

Serve with glasses of freshly squeezed orange juice and lots of buttery toast.

halloumi bacon & mushroom sandwich
with Dijon mustard and crusty sourdough

✱

A hearty, chewy, deeply satisfying breakfast sandwich with layers of smoky, marinated halloumi bacon, huge juicy garlic mushrooms, peppery watercress and Dijon mustard. All wedged between two hunks of toasted sourdough.

serves 2

25g/¼ stick butter
½ garlic clove, crushed
4 large, flat mushrooms
4 slices crusty sourdough bread
2 tablespoons Dijon mustard
2 handfuls watercress
1 recipe halloumi bacon (page 36)

Preheat the oven to 200°C/400°F. Mix together the butter and garlic and season with a big pinch of flaky salt if using unsalted butter. Arrange the mushrooms, gills down, on a baking tray and roast for 10 minutes to remove some water. Take out of the oven, spread over the butter and roast for a further 10 minutes.

Toast the bread and spread with Dijon mustard. Layer the watercress, garlic mushrooms, halloumi bacon and bread.

✱

Wedge the juicy, garlicky mushrooms and chewy halloumi bacon between the mustardy sourdough bread. And eat.

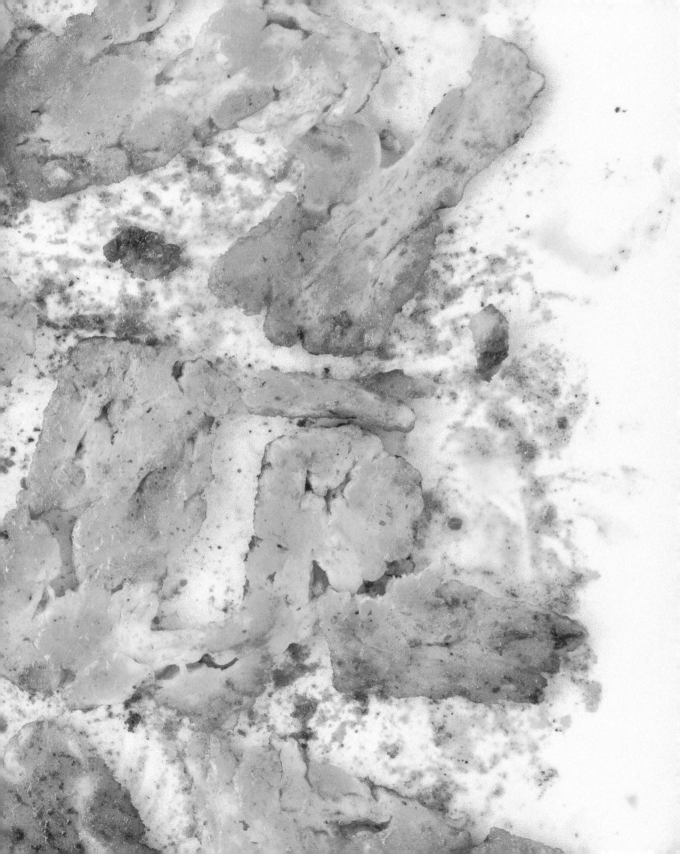

croque madame
with halloumi bacon and fried egg

✻

A smoky, meaty, cheesy sandwich fried in butter, topped with béchamel and grilled until bubbly. Sourdough, Dijon mustard, halloumi bacon, cheese sauce, melty Gruyère and a crispy fried egg – for when only the most decadent of breakfasts will do.

serves 4

halloumi and Gruyère béchamel

25g/¼ stick butter
25g/3 tablespoons plain flour
230ml/1 cup whole milk
few scrapes whole nutmeg
30g/1oz halloumi, finely grated
30g /1oz Gruyère, finely grated

In a small saucepan, melt the butter over medium heat, add the flour and cook, stirring frequently, for a few minutes. Add the milk and whisk until smooth and starting to thicken. Continue cooking for a couple of minutes, stirring frequently, until very thick and starting to pull away from the sides of the pan. Scrape in the nutmeg, stir in the cheeses until melted and set aside while you prepare the rest of the sandwich.

croque madame

8 slices crusty sourdough bread
4 tablespoons Dijon mustard
1 recipe <u>halloumi bacon (page 36)</u>
100g/1 cup + 75g/¾ cup finely grated Gruyère
40g/⅓ stick butter
1 recipe <u>béchamel (page 47)</u>
4 eggs
truffle salt to sprinkle

Making 4 sandwiches, layer 1 slice of sourdough, 1 tablespoon Dijon mustard, a quarter of the halloumi bacon, 25g/¼ cup grated Gruyère and top with another slice of bread.

Heat the butter in a large, heavy frying pan over medium heat. When the butter stops foaming, add the sandwiches, reduce the heat to medium-low and cover. Cook the sandwiches on both sides until golden brown and the cheese has melted, about 2 minutes on each side.

While the sandwiches are cooking, heat the grill. Divide the béchamel between the 4 sandwiches, spreading it over one of the toasted sides. Sprinkle over the last of the Gruyère and grill until very bubbly and lightly browned.

While the sandwiches are grilling, fry the eggs – use the frying pan you made the sandwiches in, there might even be a little browned butter left in the pan (if not, add more butter or oil). Heat the pan over medium heat until hot. Crack in the eggs, cover the pan and turn off the heat. Leave the eggs to gently steam-fry in the residual heat. The eggs are done when the top layer of egg white is cooked, but the yolk is still very runny, about 2 minutes.

✱

Top the bubbly, caramelised cheese with a crispy fried egg, sprinkle with a little truffle salt and serve.

harissa halloumi salad
with tomato pesto and avocado

✴

Chunks of salty halloumi roasted with bright, hot harissa, piled on watercress, pea shoots and creamy avocado. Seasoned with dollops of tomato pesto, super tangy pomegranate molasses, fresh mint and lemon zest. So very much flavour.

serves 4

harissa halloumi salad

1 recipe <u>harissa halloumi (overleaf)</u>
1 recipe <u>tomato pesto (overleaf)</u>
1 cucumber
1 red onion
250g/9oz cherry tomatoes
1-2 ripe avocados
few handfuls pea shoots
few handfuls watercress
4 tablespoons pomegranate molasses
good handful fresh mint
1 lemon, zest only

While the halloumi is cooking, thinly slice the cucumber and red onion (the thinner the better), halve the cherry tomatoes and cut the avocado into chunks. Layer the pea shoots, watercress and prepared vegetables on the plates. Top with the harissa halloumi and dollops of tomato pesto. Drizzle over the pomegranate molasses, sprinkle over the zest and fresh herbs and grind over plenty of pepper.

harissa halloumi

2 packs halloumi, cut into chunks
3 heaped tablespoons harissa

Add the halloumi to a baking dish and toss with the harissa. Leave to marinate while you heat the oven to 180°C/350°F. Roast for about 20 minutes, stirring once or twice to coat, until the cheese moisture has evaporated and the halloumi is very lightly browned.

tomato pesto

40g/10 dried tomato halves
1 garlic clove, crushed
½ lemon, juice only

Cover the dried tomatoes with boiling water, leave to soften for about 20 minutes. Juice the lemon, add the garlic to the juice and set aside for 20 minutes – this effectively cooks the garlic. Add the softened tomatoes, lemon and garlic to a food processor with a splash of the soak water and blend to a pesto. Taste to check for seasoning, adding a pinch of flaky salt if necessary (dried tomatoes can be salty).

✱

Sprinkle salad and herbs, dollop tomato pesto and scatter over the hot, spicy halloumi.

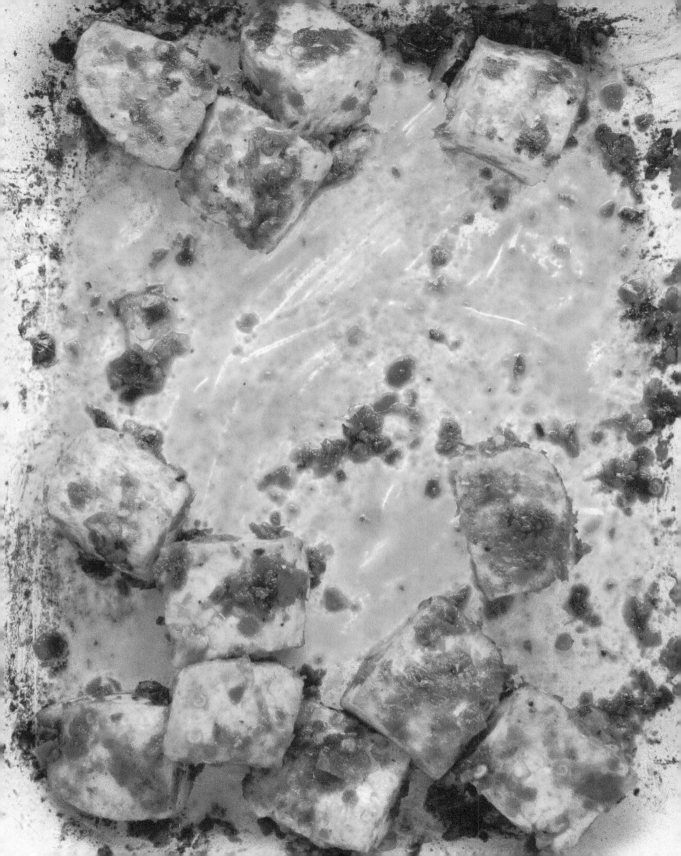

halloumi onion bhaji waffles
with poached egg and avocado

✱

Super easy breakfast waffles made with chickpea flour – an extremely delicious, healthy flour that everyone should have in their pantry. Packed with fresh onion, steamed until silky in the batter – these waffles are great with a poached egg (or two) and a few slices of creamy avocado.

serves 4/makes 4 large waffles

halloumi onion bhaji waffles

160g/1 ¾ cups chickpea flour
80g/½ cup cornflour
½ teaspoon baking powder (optional)
1 medium onion, cut into 1cm/½" dice
1 pack halloumi, half grated and half cubed
1-2 hot green chillies, finely chopped
4 teaspoons cumin seeds

Mix the flours with ½ teaspoon flaky salt and plenty of pepper. Add 120g/½ cup cold water and whisk to form a smooth batter. Stir in the onion, halloumi and green chilli.

Heat the oven to 160°C/325°F to keep the finished waffles warm and heat your waffle machine to its highest setting. When it has come to temperature, brush the inside with a little oil, pour in an appropriate amount of batter (it will depend on your machine) and scatter over 1 teaspoon cumin seeds – be careful not to overfill as this mixture expands. Close and cook until lightly browned and crisp, about 5 minutes, then ease the waffle from the machine with the point of a knife. Repeat with the rest of the batter, adding more oil as necessary, keeping the other waffles warm as you work.

poached eggs

4 very fresh eggs
truffle salt to sprinkle

Fill a medium saucepan with water, add ½ tablespoon coarse sea salt and heat to just below boiling (bubbling water isn't good for a beautiful poached egg). Crack the first egg into a small sieve to remove any loose, runny white and tip the rest of the egg into the water. Repeat with the other eggs, trying to space them evenly in the pan.

Start checking if the eggs are done after a couple of minutes by lifting one out with a slotted spoon and giving it a little wobble – you can see which bits might need more cooking. My egg is done when all the white around the yolk is just set and the yolk is still soft and very runny.

to serve

2 ripe avocados
squeeze of lemon juice
handful fresh mint, coriander or parsley

Peel, slice and season the avocado with a squeeze of lemon and a little flaky salt.

✴

Pile the warm, crispy waffles with avocado slices, poached eggs and herbs and serve immediately.

cheese toastie
with halloumi, Stilton and Gruyère

✳

A snack for private moments, for five minutes of melty, cheesy, umami joy when all that matters is your sandwich and how many bites you have left. Toasted sourdough, mustard and a layer of smoky halloumi surrounded by melty Stilton and earthy Gruyère.

serves 1

2 slices crusty sourdough bread
1 teaspoon Dijon mustard
25g/¼ cup finely grated Gruyère
2 slices halloumi bacon (page 36) or 2 thin slices halloumi
15g/⅛ cup crumbled Stilton
10 sprigs thyme, leaves only
a little butter

Spread the bread with the Dijon mustard and layer the Gruyère, halloumi and Stilton. Sprinkle over the thyme leaves and season with lots of pepper. Butter the outer sides of the bread and toast the sandwich on both sides – I use a medium-hot cast iron frying pan with something heavy pressing on it (or a waffle machine if I'm feeling jaunty).

✳

Serve without interruptions.

dinner

dinner

dinner

*

rich, spicy tomato curry
with mushroom, halloumi and brown basmati 66

macaroni & cheese
with halloumi bacon and the cheesiest of sauces 70

courgette & halloumi burgers
with basil pesto and lemony asparagus 74

palak halloumi
with brown butter parathas 78

tomato risotto
with roasted halloumi, cherry tomatoes and garlic 82

pumpkin, potato & halloumi gratin
with romaine salad and cider vinaigrette 86

harissa halloumi kebabs
with spelt-avocado wraps 90

crispy halloumi chipotle burgers
with avocado and watercress salad 94

halloumi cannelloni
with spinach, cavolo nero and crème fraîche 98

marinated halloumi in vine leaves
with barberry freekeh and tomato-avocado salad 102

*

Taking time for each other.

rich, spicy tomato curry
with halloumi, mushroom and brown basmati

✳

Inspired by the cooking of Kaushy Patel, a woman responsible for some of the best vegetarian food in Britain today – a buttery, spicy tomato sauce, simmered with sweetly caramelised onions, earthy mushrooms and soft chunks of salty halloumi. Served with nutty brown basmati rice, creamy yoghurt and handfuls of fresh, lemony coriander.

serves 4

spicy tomato curry with halloumi

250g/9oz chestnut mushrooms, quartered
1 large onion, peeled and ends removed
6cm/2" piece of ginger, peeled and finely grated to a pulp
3 hot green chillies, finely sliced
6 garlic cloves, crushed
2 tins/28oz tomatoes
1 teaspoon turmeric
2 teaspoons ground coriander
1 teaspoon ground cumin
40g/⅓ stick butter
½ teaspoon garam masala
1 pack halloumi, cubed in 2cm/1" chunks

Heat a heavy frying pan over medium heat (no need to add oil). When the pan is hot, arrange the mushrooms in an even layer. Cook until browned on that side, then stir and repeat, cooking on all sides until evenly browned. Season with ¼ teaspoon flaky salt and set aside.

Add the onion to a food processor and blend to a purée, scraping down as needed.

Heat a good drizzle of oil in a large saucepan over medium heat until hot. Add the chillies and garlic, stir until fragrant, about 30 seconds. Add the onion and stir to combine. Caramelise the onion purée by leaving it undisturbed until it starts to brown, then stir and repeat until it is all dark and well caramelised – this process should take at least 10 minutes.

When the onion is ready, add the tomatoes, ginger, turmeric, ground coriander, ground cumin and 2 teaspoons flaky salt. Blend with an immersion blender to break down the tomatoes and bring the sauce together and simmer for a few minutes. Add the butter and 100g/7 tablespoons boiling water and simmer over a low heat for about 10 minutes, until the sauce thickens and everything is cooked.

Turn off the heat and stir in the garam masala, halloumi and cooked mushrooms, cover and rest for 15 minutes.

baked brown basmati rice

250g/1 ½ cups brown basmati rice
25g/¼ stick butter

Heat the oven to 180°C/350°F. Add the rice to a large baking dish and scatter over 1 teaspoon flaky salt. Add 650g/2 ½ cups boiling water to the rice, drizzle over a little oil and stir to combine evenly. Wrap well in foil, put in the oven carefully and bake for 1 hour.

Remove from the oven, uncover and fluff with a fork. Cut the butter into small cubes and dot over. Stir the butter through, cover with a clean tea towel and rest for 5-10 minutes.

to serve

2 big handfuls fresh coriander, leaves and stems, chopped
250g/8oz Greek yoghurt

Reheat the curry briefly, if needed, and sprinkle over the fresh coriander.

✶

Serve piled onto fluffy, buttery basmati rice with big dollops of cooling Greek yoghurt.

macaroni & cheese

with halloumi bacon and the cheesiest of sauces

★

More cheese flavour in one bite than you ever thought possible. Starting with a base of umami tomato stock, this recipe builds layer upon layer of cheesy deliciousness – baked until bubbly with crumbled halloumi bacon, melted blue cheese and nutty Gruyère.

serves 4

the cheesiest of sauces

3 dried tomato halves
300g/10oz pasta, whatever shape you fancy
1 tablespoon truffle oil or butter
1 teaspoon nutritional yeast
½ pack halloumi, finely grated
50g/½ cup finely grated Gruyère cheese
1 very lightly heaped tablespoon cornflour
100g/½ cup cream cheese

Add the dried tomatoes to a saucepan with 400g/1 ¾ cups boiling water and soak for 30 minutes. Blend thoroughly with an immersion blender to create a tomato vegetable stock and season with ½ teaspoon flaky salt.

While the tomatoes are soaking, cook the pasta. Heat 600g/2 ½ cups water and 1 teaspoon flaky salt until close to the boil, add the pasta and stir to coat. Cover and simmer on a low heat, stirring every few minutes to stop everything sticking, until the pasta is cooked to your liking – usually 25% longer than the packet instructions with this method. When the pasta is ready, remove from the heat – don't worry if there's a little liquid left, this is pure starchy gold. Toss with the truffle oil or butter, cover and set aside.

Toss the halloumi and Gruyère with the cornflour. Heat the stock over medium heat, stir through the cornflour-coated cheeses and cook until the cheese is melted and incorporated (the halloumi won't completely melt) and the sauce bubbles and thickens. Stir through the pasta, cream cheese and plenty of pepper.

assembly

1 recipe <u>halloumi bacon (page 36)</u>
50g/½ cup Stilton or other blue cheese
50g/½ cup finely grated Gruyère

Preheat the oven to 180°C/350°F. Layer half the pasta in a baking dish, then crumble over the halloumi bacon and blue cheese, followed by the rest of the pasta. Top with the remaining Gruyère.

Bake for about 20 minutes, until everything is fully warmed through and the cheese topping is lightly browned and crispy.

✳

Serve with glasses of dry sparkling wine to cut the gorgeous richness.

courgette & halloumi burgers
with lemon asparagus and basil pesto

✱

Moist shreds of courgette, packed into a veggie burger with chunks of halloumi, lemon and fresh herbs – baked, not fried, so extra light and healthy. Dolloped with fresh basil pesto and sandwiched in a crusty bun, served with sautéed, lemony asparagus.

serves 4

courgette and halloumi burgers

1kg/6 small courgettes
1 medium onion, cut in 1cm/½" dice
4 garlic cloves, crushed
1 pack halloumi, cut in small cubes
1 lemon, juice and zest
2 large handfuls fresh herbs
¼ teaspoon hot chilli powder
1 egg, lightly beaten
2 heaped tablespoons chickpea flour

Grate the courgettes into a colander, sprinkle evenly with 1 teaspoon flaky salt and toss to combine. Leave to drain for about an hour. Pile half the grated courgette in the middle of a clean tea towel and twist around the courgette to remove as much water as possible.

Preheat the oven to 200°C/400°F. Add the squeezed courgettes to a large bowl and mix through the rest of the ingredients with 1 teaspoon flaky salt and plenty of pepper. Shape the mixture into 4 large patties and lay on baking paper or a non-stick baking tray (don't use foil, it sticks!).

Bake for about 40 minutes, until they are brown all over, carefully turning over each patty about halfway through (a metal spatula is best). Allow to cool for 20 minutes to firm up.

basil pesto

big handful fresh basil, leaves only
good squeeze of lemon juice
1 garlic clove
100ml/7 tablespoons cold-pressed oil

In a food processor, add the basil and lemon juice and whizz to finely chop. Add the garlic and ½ teaspoon flaky salt and blend again, drizzling in the oil and blending to a smooth sauce. Press plastic wrap against the exposed pesto (to prevent discolouring) and set aside until needed.

lemon asparagus

300g/10oz asparagus
½ lemon, juice only
25g/¼ stick butter

Snap off the woody ends of the asparagus. Heat a good drizzle of oil over medium heat in a heavy frying pan until hot. Add the asparagus in an even layer and cover for a couple of minutes, steam-frying, then stir and cover again until just tender. Turn off the heat, add the lemon and butter and season with ½ teaspoon flaky salt and plenty of pepper, stirring to combine. Serve immediately.

to serve

4 crusty sourdough rolls, halved
4 tablespoons Greek yoghurt
100g/4oz lettuce or salad leaves
½ red onion, finely sliced

While the asparagus is cooking, spread the rolls with yoghurt and the other with some of the pesto. Rewarm the cooled courgette patties and layer lettuce, patties and red onion.

✱

Serve with the citrussy asparagus and dollops of basil pesto.

palak halloumi
with brown butter parathas

★

Soft, chewy, tender chunks of halloumi, simmered in a creamy, garlicky spinach sauce. Served with cooling yoghurt and parathas – the puff pastry of the flatbread world – with their flaky brown butter layers. All kinds of delicious.

serves 4

palak halloumi

1 onion, peeled, ends trimmed
600g/1lb 5oz fresh spinach
good squeeze of lemon juice
3 hot green chillies, finely sliced
5 garlic cloves, crushed
1 teaspoon fenugreek seeds
1 teaspoon cumin seeds
½ teaspoon turmeric
2 teaspoons ground coriander
pinch of asafoetida
1 teaspoon garam masala
1 pack halloumi, cut into 2cm/1" cubes, brine reserved
drizzle of double cream

Add the onion to a food processor and purée, scraping down as needed. Set aside. Heat a large pan of boiling water with 1 tablespoon coarse sea salt, blanch the spinach for 1 minute and shock in cold water – this helps fix the green colour. Drain the spinach and add to the food processor, blending to a purée with the lemon juice, sliced chillies and 1 clove of crushed garlic. Set aside.

Heat a good drizzle of oil in a large saucepan over medium heat until hot and fry the fenugreek and cumin seeds until they start to pop. Add the onion purée and stir to combine. Caramelise the onion by leaving it undisturbed until it starts to brown, then stir and repeat until it is all well caramelised – this should take at least 10 minutes.

When the onion is ready, add the rest of the garlic and cook until fragrant, about 2 minutes. Add the turmeric, ground coriander and asafoetida and cook for a few seconds. Add the spinach purée and 100g/7 tablespoons water and simmer on low for 5 minutes – the sauce should be thick, but add more water if you want it thinner. Add the cheese and its brine to the spinach sauce. Stir through the garam masala, cream and 1 teaspoon flaky salt, cover and rest for 10 minutes. Check the seasoning before serving.

brown butter parathas

100g/1 stick butter
300g/2 ⅓ cups whole grain spelt or atta flour

Add the butter to a small saucepan and heat over medium-low heat until the milk solids caramelise and the butter is dark golden-brown.

Add the flour and 1 teaspoon flaky salt to a food processor and whizz to combine. Drizzle in half the melted butter and blend to combine well. With the machine running, add enough boiling water (about 100g/7 tablespoons, depending on your flour) to form a supple dough that is not sticky. Blend for 1-2 minutes to knead the dough, until it is smooth, soft and a little shiny. Cover with plastic wrap and rest for at least 10 minutes.

Roll the paratha using the brown butter to make the flaky layers. Heat a large, heavy frying pan over medium heat until very hot (you don't need any extra oil). Add a rolled paratha to the pan – it should bubble in about a minute and be spotted brown on the heated side. If it takes much longer than that, the paratha will dry out before it browns and become tough and inflexible, so adjust the heat accordingly. Flip the paratha and cook for another minute to brown the other side. Keep the cooked parathas soft as you work by wrapping the stack in a clean, lightly damp tea towel.

to serve

250g/8oz Greek yoghurt
1 lemon, cut into wedges

✱

Serve with the hot bread, lemon wedges for squeezing and big dollops of cooling Greek yoghurt.

making the buttery layers

Divide the dough into 8 pieces – keep the dough balls covered in plastic wrap while you work. Roll 1 dough ball into a 20cm/8" round. Brush brown butter evenly over the dough round and sprinkle over a tiny bit of flour. Roll another 20cm/8" round and lay over the first. Fold the edges of the dough into the centre, making a rough hexagon. Turn the package over, sprinkle with a little more flour and roll out again into a 20cm/8" round.

tomato risotto
with roasted halloumi, tomatoes and garlic

✱

A scrumptious tomato risotto flavoured with rich, umami tomato paste. Topped with herby halloumi, cherry tomatoes and whole garlic cloves, roasted until tender and juicy in a low oven. Melt-in-the-mouth amazing.

serves 4

tomato risotto

70g/15-20 dried tomatoes halves
1 onion, cut into 1cm/½" dice
4 garlic cloves, crushed
400g/2 cups risotto rice
medium glass white wine
1400g/6 cups vegetable stock
40g/⅓ stick butter, cut into small cubes
75g/⅔ cup finely grated Parmesan
big handful fresh basil, leaves only

Cover the dried tomatoes with boiling water and leave to soften for about 30 minutes. Blend to a purée with a splash of the soak water and set aside. In a large saucepan, bring the vegetable stock to the boil, then turn down the heat to keep just hot.

Heat another large saucepan (for the risotto) with a good drizzle of oil over medium heat until hot. Add the diced onion and sauté until softened and translucent, about 5 minutes. Stir through the garlic and cook for a couple of minutes, until fragrant. Add the rice and sauté for a few more minutes, then add the white wine and stir until absorbed. Add three-quarters of the stock and stir to combine. Turn the heat down to low, cover and simmer until the rice is al dente, about 15 minutes, stirring occasionally (this is a mostly hands-free risotto method).

Add the blended tomatoes and remaining stock to the rice and stir vigorously for 2 minutes, until the rice is tender and creamy. Taste for seasoning, then stir through the butter, Parmesan and basil. Remove from the heat, cover and rest for 10 minutes.

roasted halloumi, cherry tomatoes and garlic

200g/7oz cherry tomatoes
1 head garlic, cloves peeled
1 sprig rosemary, leaves only, finely chopped
1 pack halloumi, cut in 2cm/1" chunks

Preheat oven to 180°C/350°F. Put all the ingredients except the halloumi in an ovenproof dish and drizzle over a little oil. Bake until the garlic is soft, about 20 minutes.

Add the halloumi and stir to combine. Roast for further 5 minutes, until the cheese is lightly browned.

✶

Serve with the roasted halloumi, cherry tomatoes and garlic cloves spooned over the top.

potato, pumpkin & halloumi gratin
with romaine salad and cider vinaigrette

★

A luxurious gratin with colourful layers of sweet orange pumpkin, salty white halloumi and tender potato, baked in pumpkin stock and a little cream. The fresh, tart salad lightens and brightens the meal, balancing the cream. Excellent with a glass or two of dry apple cider.

serves 4

potato, pumpkin and halloumi gratin

500g/½ small pumpkin or butternut squash
2 garlic cloves, crushed
300ml/½ pint double cream
⅛ whole nutmeg, freshly grated
6 fresh sage leaves, finely chopped
600g/4 medium potatoes
1 pack halloumi

Preheat the oven to 180°C/350°F. Peel, halve and deseed the squash, adding all the trimmings to a medium saucepan. Add the crushed garlic and 600g/2 ½ cups water, bring to the boil and simmer for 20 minutes. Strain the stock to remove the squash trimmings, pressing with a spatula to extract the most flavour – you will be left with about 400g/1 ¾ cups stock. Add the cream, nutmeg, sage and ½ teaspoon flaky salt and plenty of pepper – the sauce should be flavourful and fairly salty.

While the stock is simmering, thinly slice the pumpkin, potatoes and halloumi. Starting with a little sauce, layer potatoes, pumpkin and halloumi, separating each layer with a couple more tablespoons of sauce – keep the pieces overlapping but fairly loose so the liquid will be able to penetrate. Finish with a layer of pumpkin and a covering of sauce – make sure there is at least 1cm/½" left at the top to allow for bubbling up. Cover with foil and bake for 40-50 minutes, until the vegetables feel tender when poked with a knife. Remove the foil and bake for a further 10 minutes to brown the top. Grind on a generous helping of pepper and rest for 10 minutes before serving.

romaine salad with cider vinaigrette

1 head romaine lettuce
1 tablespoon Dijon mustard
2 tablespoons apple cider vinegar
100ml/7 tablespoons cold-pressed oil

You can whisk the dressing ingredients together by hand, but if you prefer a creamy, emulsified dressing, a food processor or blender is best. Start with the mustard, vinegar, ½ teaspoon flaky salt and lots of pepper, then add the oil in a drizzle – blend until the dressing is thick and smooth.

＊

Serve the creamy, delicately sweet gratin – with its beautiful orange and white layers – alongside the tangy green salad.

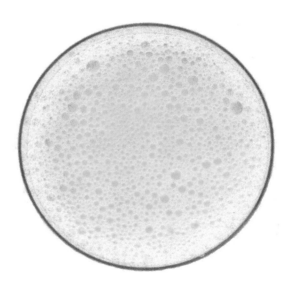

harissa halloumi kebabs
with spelt-avocado wraps

✶

Whole grain spelt flour is healthy, nutty and delicious and a hot, heavy frying pan is all you need to have fresh bread on the table in minutes. Pile the wraps with soft, spicy chunks of halloumi caramelised with harissa, roasted vegetables and other tasty bits and pieces.

serves 4

roasted mushrooms and leeks

4 large, flat mushrooms, sliced
1 leek, thinly sliced

Preheat the oven to 180°C/350°F. Add the vegetables to a baking dish and stir through a little oil. Roast for 30 minutes, stirring once, until the vegetables are well cooked and browned in places. Season with ½ teaspoon flaky salt and lots of pepper.

harissa halloumi

2 packs halloumi, cut into chunks
3 heaped tablespoons harissa

Add the halloumi to a baking dish and toss with the harissa. Roast for about 20 minutes (time this to go with the vegetables), stirring once or twice to coat, until the cheese moisture has evaporated and the halloumi is very lightly browned.

spelt-avocado wraps

250g/2 cups whole grain spelt flour
1 medium ripe avocado

Add the flour, avocado and 1 teaspoon flaky salt to a food processor and blend to cut the avocado into the flour – there should be no lumps. With the machine running, add enough boiling water (about 90g/6 tablespoons, it depends on your flour) to form a soft, supple dough that is not sticky. Continue blending for 1-2 minutes to knead the dough, until it is smooth and a little shiny. Cover in plastic wrap and rest for at least 10 minutes.

Heat a large, heavy frying pan over medium heat until very hot (you don't need any oil). Divide the dough into 8 pieces, keeping the waiting dough balls covered with plastic wrap to stop them drying out. Roll the first wrap about 20cm/8" wide and add to the pan – it should bubble in about a minute and be spotted brown on the heated side. If it takes much longer than that, the wrap will dry out before it browns and become tough and inflexible, so adjust the heat accordingly. Flip the wrap and cook for another minute to brown the other side. Keep the cooked wraps soft as you work by wrapping the stack in a clean, lightly damp tea towel.

to serve

1 red onion, very thinly sliced
1 big handful mixed salad leaves
1 big handful herbs
250g/8oz Greek yoghurt
1 lemon, cut into wedges

✳

Serve so everyone can make their own kebabs, piling hot, roasted harissa halloumi and vegetables on the nutty spelt wraps, with creamy yoghurt and tart squeezes of lemon.

crispy halloumi chipotle burgers
with avocado and watercress salad

✱

Wedges of soft, chewy halloumi marinated in smoky chipotle chilli and shallow-fried in a super crispy batter. A fabulously satisfying veggie burger with hot, crunchy cheese and red onion, squished in a crusty sourdough bun. Served with fresh watercress, creamy avocado and a zingy shallot dressing.

serves 4

crispy chipotle halloumi

2 packs halloumi
3 chipotles in adobo or 3 tablespoons chipotle paste
60g/½ cup plain flour
40g/¼ cup cornflour
60ml/4 tablespoons oil

Split the halloumi along its natural crack and divide each cheese into two large rectangles. Cut those large rectangles into two smaller rectangles, so you are left with 8 flat rectangles of cheese. Pat the cheese dry with a paper towel. Blend or crush the chipotles into a paste if necessary and rub all over the pieces of cheese. Season with lots of pepper and leave to marinate while you prepare the batter.

Combine the flours in a medium bowl with a good pinch of flaky salt and whisk in about 120g/½ cup cold water – enough to make a smooth, lump-free batter the consistency of double cream. Heat the oil in a large, heavy frying pan over medium heat until hot. Dip one piece of cheese into the batter, drip off any excess and add to the frying pan. Repeat with more cheese, filling the pan, but not overcrowding – you may need to do this in batches. Cook until browned on both sides, flipping halfway through – you may need to add a little extra oil. Drain briefly on paper towels and serve while still piping hot.

avocado and watercress salad

1 shallot, finely chopped
2 tablespoons apple cider vinegar
1 tablespoon honey
4 tablespoons cold-pressed oil
200g/7oz watercress
2 ripe avocados

Add the chopped shallot to the vinegar and set aside for 20 minutes – this effectively cooks the shallot. When you are ready to serve, add the watercress to a large serving bowl. Peel and chop the avocados into chunks and add to the watercress. Whisk the honey into the vinegar and shallot mixture, then the oil and season with a big pinch of flaky salt and a few screws of pepper. Toss the salad with the dressing and serve immediately.

to serve

4 crusty sourdough rolls, halved
4 tablespoons whole grain mustard
2 big handfuls salad leaves
1 red onion, finely sliced
handful mustard cress

Spread the mustard on the rolls and layer the salad leaves, crispy halloumi, red onion and mustard cress.

*

Pile the cheesy burgers high with toppings and serve the tangy watercress salad alongside.

halloumi cannelloni
with spinach, cavolo nero and crème fraîche

✱

Stuffed with masses of spinach and cavolo nero, wilted down with garlic, lemon and herbs. With delicate layers of homemade pasta and halloumi, wrapped around the filling in a tasty, cheesy tube. Leave the odd bit of halloumi poking out of the cannelloni ends – it caramelises beautifully.

serves 4

cannelloni filling

200g/7oz cavolo nero
400g/14oz fresh spinach
handful fresh parsley, leaves only
handful fresh basil, leaves only
1 teaspoon dried oregano
1 garlic clove, crushed
squeeze of fresh lemon juice
2 eggs

Bring a large pot of water to the boil with 1 tablespoon coarse sea salt. Strip the leaves from the cavolo nero by holding the stem with one hand and stripping the leaves off either side with the other. Cut into 5cm/2" pieces and blanch for about 5 minutes, until just tender. Remove from the water with a slotted spoon and run under cool water to stop the cooking.

Add the spinach to the water (do this in 2 batches) and cook until just wilted, about 1 minute. Remove from the water with a slotted spoon and add to a colander. Run under cool water to stop the cooking – reserve the hot water for cooking the pasta sheets.

Pile about a third of the greens in a clean tea towel and twist to squeeze out as much water as possible. Repeat with the rest of the greens, roughly chop and add to a large bowl. Roughly chop the fresh herbs and stir through with the oregano, garlic, lemon, eggs, 1 teaspoon flaky salt and lots of pepper.

fresh egg pasta

100g/¾ cup strong white bread flour
100g/¾ cup strong whole wheat bread flour
2 large eggs
fine semolina, for dusting

Add the flours and eggs to a food processor or other mixer and blend into a dough. In a food processor this takes 2-3 minutes, in a stand mixer or other machine that kneads, about 10 minutes. Remove from the machine, knead a few times to check it isn't sticky (sprinkle flour as needed) and shape into a ball. Cover in plastic wrap and rest for at least 30 minutes.

Roll the pasta sheets medium thin, about setting 5-6 on a pasta machine. Bring the reserved blanching water to the boil and cook the sheets for 5 minutes, until just tender. Rinse under cold water and set aside, laid flat, until you are ready to fill.

assembly

1 pack halloumi, thinly sliced
300ml/10oz crème fraîche
60g/⅔ cup finely grated Gruyère cheese
few scrapes whole nutmeg

Preheat the oven to 180°C/350°F and butter a large baking dish. Mix the crème fraîche with a couple of tablespoons of milk or water to loosen. Spread out one cooked pasta sheet and lay three pieces of halloumi next to each other at one end. Cover with 3 tablespoons filling and dollop on 1 teaspoon crème fraîche. Roll the edge of the pasta over the filling with a little overlap and cut off the rest of the pasta sheet. Lay the filled cannelloni roll in the baking dish. Repeat with the rest of the fillings. Smooth the remaining crème fraîche over the top, sprinkle over the Gruyère and bake until golden and bubbly, 20-30 minutes, turning once so it cooks evenly. Finish with a little pepper and a few scrapes of nutmeg.

✱

Serve with a glass of fruity sauvignon blanc.

kneading and rolling the pasta sheets

Cut the dough into 4 slices, as you would a loaf of bread. Shape 1 piece into a rough rectangle and feed through a pasta machine on setting 1, keeping everything dusted with semolina. Fold the pasta in half and run through the machine again, repeating this process until you hear a loud pop as the last bit of folded pasta passes through the rollers.

Continue running the pasta through the machine, increasing the setting a stage at a time until the pasta is the required thinness. Lay the sheets on a work surface dusted with semolina.

marinated halloumi in vine leaves
with barberry freekeh and tomato salad

✳

This dish is a variation of a recipe I saw in Sirocco, Sabrina Gayour's absolutely gorgeous cookbook – truly one of the best cookbooks I've ever seen. Halloumi marinated in chilli, lemon and garlic, wrapped in vine leaves and baked until soft and juicy. Served with buttery whole grain freekeh, a juicy tomato-avocado salad, creamy Greek yoghurt and romaine leaves for scooping everything up.

serves 4

marinated halloumi in vine leaves

1 pack halloumi
10 vine leaves in brine
1 teaspoon <u>habanero oil (page 121)</u>
small handful fresh herbs, chopped
1 lemon, zest only
1 garlic clove, crushed

Soak the vine leaves for 10 minutes in cold water to remove some of the saltiness. Split the halloumi in half along its natural break so you have two flat rectangles.

Spread out 3 vine leaves, (overlapping in places to make a larger layer), lay 1 rectangle of halloumi on the leaves and spread over half the seasonings and a few screws of pepper. Lay over 2 more vine leaves, wrap the package as best you can and lay on a baking tray with any loose edges facing down. Repeat with the other piece of halloumi and the remaining vine leaves and seasonings.

Bake together with the freekeh (overleaf) for the last 30 minutes of cooking.

barberry and parsley freekeh

225g/1 cup freekeh
25g/¼ stick butter, cut into small cubes
2 handfuls dried barberries
2 handfuls fresh parsley, leaves only, chopped

Preheat the oven to 180°C/350°F. Add the freekeh to a large baking dish and scatter over 1 teaspoon flaky salt. Add 550g/2 ⅓ cups boiling water, drizzle over a little oil and stir to combine evenly. Wrap well in foil and bake for 1 hour.

Uncover and check the freekeh is tender. If there is any excess water (it depends on your freekeh), remove the foil and return to the oven to dry out. When the freekeh is ready, take out of the oven and fluff with a fork. Dot over the butter and stir through the barberries and parsley. Cover with a tea towel and rest for 10 minutes before serving.

tomato-avocado salad

1 lemon, juice only
1 garlic clove, crushed
200g/7oz cherry tomatoes, quartered
2 ripe avocados

Juice the lemon, add the garlic to the juice and set aside for 20 minutes – this effectively cooks the garlic. Add the cut tomatoes to a colander, stir through ½ teaspoon flaky salt and leave to drain for 20 minutes. Cut the avocado into small chunks and gently toss with the tomatoes, lemon and garlic mixture, ½ teaspoon flaky salt and lots of pepper.

to serve

250g/8oz Greek yoghurt
½ head romaine, leaves separated

✶

Pile nutty grains, tender cheese and juicy salad on romaine leaves and drizzle over yoghurt.

party!

party!

party!

✳

halloumi fries
with garlic mayonnaise 112

halloumi choux pastry fritters
with tomato and basil 116

habanero oil halloumi
with spelt za'atar crackers 120

spinach & halloumi pie
with filo pastry 124

battered halloumi & chips
with lemon pickled onions and coriander peas 130

roasted aubergine & halloumi pizza
with crème fraîche and nigella seed crust 136

spring greens & halloumi pizza
with fresh red chilli and oregano crust 140

broccoli & halloumi pizza
with pickled chillies and sumac crust 142

chewy, crunchy, nutty pizza dough
with a thin, crispy base and puffed, airy crust 146

halloumi & spinach tamales
with guacamole, chipotle cream and coriander salad 152

butternut squash & halloumi Wellington
with winter vegetables, Yorkshire pudding and garlic sauce 158

✳

The joy of sharing food.

halloumi fries
with garlic mayonnaise

*

Make friends and influence people with these sensational party snacks – deep-fried halloumi with a crispy, earthy nigella seed batter. Dip in bright, lemony garlic mayonnaise for inappropriate levels of cheesy enjoyment.

serves 4-6

crispy halloumi fries

100g/1 cup chickpea flour
40g/⅓ cup cornflour
4 level tablespoons nigella seeds
2 packs halloumi, cut into long strips
1 litre/1 quart frying oil
1 lemon, cut into wedges

Whisk together the flours, nigella seeds, ½ teaspoon flaky salt and 140g/⅔ cup cold water – the batter should have the consistency of double cream.

Preheat the oven to 160°C/325°F to keep the fries warm as you cook them in batches. Cover a baking tray with 2 layers of kitchen towel to soak up any excess oil. Heat the oil in a large pan to 170°C/350°F – if you don't have a thermometer, at this temperature a cube of bread will brown in 45-60 seconds.

Coat a piece of halloumi in the batter and drip off any excess. Carefully slide into the oil and repeat with about 8 more fries – any more and the pan will become too crowded and the oil temperature will drop. Fry for about 5 minutes, until lightly browned and very crispy. Drain on the baking tray and keep hot in the oven while you finish frying the rest of the cheese.

garlic mayonnaise

½ lemon, juice only
1 garlic clove, crushed
2 egg yolks
230ml/1 cup cold-pressed oil

Juice the lemon, add the garlic to the lemon juice and set aside for 20 minutes – this effectively cooks the garlic. When the garlic is ready, add to a food processor with the egg yolks and a pinch of flaky salt. Whizz for a few seconds, then start adding the oil – drip in one tiny drop at a time until the yolks have absorbed about a third of the oil and the mayonnaise has started to emulsify. If you add the oil any quicker, the mayonnaise may split.

Add the garlic, half the lemon and ¼ teaspoon flaky salt and whizz to combine. Taste to check the seasoning, adding more lemon juice or salt as needed. Loosen with a 1-2 tablespoons water if the mayonnaise is too thick.

✴

Serve the hot fries immediately, dipped in luscious garlic mayonnaise with squeezes of lemon juice.

halloumi choux pastry fritters
with tomato and basil

✳

Deep-fried choux pastry dough studded with halloumi, dried tomatoes and fresh basil –
oozy fritters that are crisp on the outside with a creamy, melty centre.

serves 4-6

halloumi choux pastry fritters

1 recipe <u>choux pastry (overleaf)</u>
30g/8 dried tomato halves
1 garlic clove, crushed
handful fresh basil, leaves only, finely chopped
1 heaped teaspoon whole grain mustard
½ pack halloumi, finely grated
1 litre/1 quart frying oil

Cover the dried tomatoes with boiling water, leave to soften for about 30 minutes, then
finely chop. Scrape the choux pastry dough into a large bowl and add the chopped
tomatoes, garlic, basil, mustard, grated halloumi, ½ teaspoon flaky sea salt and plenty of
pepper.

Preheat the oven to 160°C/325°F to keep the fritters warm as you cook them in batches.
Cover a baking tray with 2 layers of kitchen towel to soak up any excess oil. Heat the oil
in a large pan to 170°C/350°F – if you don't have a thermometer, at this temperature a
cube of bread will brown in 45-60 seconds.

Slide 1 rounded tablespoon of batter into the hot oil, repeating with 7-8 more fritters –
any more and the pan will become too crowded and the oil temperature will drop. If
they start to stick together, gently poke them apart. Fry until deep brown, about 5
minutes, turning occasionally in the oil so they cook evenly. Remove with a slotted spoon
and drain on the baking tray, keeping hot while you finish frying the rest.

choux pastry

140g/1 cup + 2 tablespoons strong white bread flour
100g/1 stick butter
5 medium eggs

Measure the flour into a bowl, add ½ teaspoon flaky sea salt and lots of pepper and set aside. Add the butter and 300g/1 ¼ cups water to a medium-large saucepan over a medium heat and bring to the boil.

As soon as it boils, turn off the heat. Tip in the flour, all in one go, and quickly beat the mixture together with a wooden spoon or electric whisk. Keep mixing until the dough is lump-free and has formed a ball which pulls away from the sides of the pan.

Whisk the eggs together in a separate bowl. Add the egg a little at a time, beating until each addition is fully incorporated – you can do this by hand, but it's much easier to move to a food processor for this stage. When the mixture is ready, it will be shiny and smooth – it should have enough body to hold its shape when dolloped, but not thicker than that. Adjust with more egg if too thick.

Press plastic wrap onto the surface to stop it forming a skin while you prepare the fritters.

✷

Serve immediately with a lovely dry cava or French crémant to help balance the cheesy richness.

habanero oil halloumi
with spelt za'atar crackers

✳

Chunks of salty halloumi cured in fruity, super spicy habanero chilli oil. Pile onto easy spelt crackers flavoured with herby za'atar – extremely zingy! This beautiful chilli oil can be used for all kinds of applications, so be sure not to throw away the curing oil – sprinkle it over everything...

serves 4-6/makes 2 small jars

habanero chilli oil

230ml/1 cup cold-pressed rapeseed oil (for the best colour)
8 fresh habanero chillies (they are very hot!!)
1 lightly heaped tablespoon smoked paprika

Slice the chillies in half lengthways, no need to deseed – wear plastic gloves if possible, as these chillies are extremely hot. Add to a saucepan with the oil and paprika. Heat on a very low heat for about 30 minutes, then turn off the heat and leave to cool to room temperature. Strain through a fine sieve to remove the chillies and paprika – you can blend these remnants into a spicy purée and save for another use (if that appeals) or discard. Season the oil with ½ teaspoon flaky salt – this will really lift the chilli flavours.

habanero oil halloumi

2 packs halloumi, cut into small cubes
1 recipe <u>habanero chilli oil</u>

Pat the halloumi cubes dry with paper towel. Layer chilli oil and halloumi chunks into 2 small jars, gently wedging in the cheese and filling any gaps as best you can. Ensure the cheese is covered with a final layer of oil. Marinate in the fridge for at least 24 hours, up to 3 weeks.

spelt za'atar crackers

200g/1 ½ cups whole grain spelt flour
6 tablespoons za'atar

Add the flour to a food processor with a good pinch of flaky salt. With the machine running, add enough boiling water (about 80g/⅓ cup, depending on your flour) to form a supple dough that is not sticky. Continue blending for 1-2 minutes to knead the dough, until it is smooth, soft and a little shiny. Cover with plastic wrap and rest for at least 10 minutes.

Roll out the dough with a pasta machine, as you would for pasta (see **Kneading and rolling the pasta sheets**, page 101) and lay the resulting cracker sheets over several baking trays. Brush with a little water, sprinkle over the za'atar and bake for 10-15 minutes, until thoroughly dried out, lightly browned and very crispy. Serve whole for diners to break into pieces as needed.

to serve

350g/12oz Greek yoghurt

✳

Serve with a bowl of Greek yoghurt on hand to cool down that super hot habanero chilli.

spinach & halloumi pie
with filo pastry

✶

Delicate layers of moist, tender filo pastry stuffed with spinach, strands of salty halloumi and fresh herbs. A fantastic party pie or splendid summer picnic nibble.

serves 6-8/makes 1 x 30cm/12" tart

spinach and halloumi filling

300g/10oz fresh spinach
big handful fresh basil, thyme or parsley, leaves only
1 pack halloumi, grated
1 egg
big squeeze of lemon juice
1 teaspoon dried oregano
big pinch hot chilli powder

Bring a large pot of water to the boil with 1 tablespoon coarse sea salt, add the spinach (do this in two batches) and cook until just wilted, about 1 minute. Drain and rinse until cool.

Pile about half the greens in a clean tea towel and twist to squeeze out as much water as possible. Repeat with the rest of the spinach, roughly chop and add to a large bowl.

Chop the fresh herbs and add to the spinach with the halloumi, egg, lemon juice, oregano, chilli powder and plenty of pepper. Mix well with a fork, taste and adjust the seasoning if necessary and set aside until you are ready to fill the pie.

filo pastry

200g/1 ½ cups strong white bread flour
cornflour, for dusting

Add the flour and ½ teaspoon flaky salt to a food processor. With the machine running, add enough boiling water (about 125g/½ cup, depending on your flour) to form a supple dough that is not sticky. Continue blending for 1-2 minutes to knead the dough, until it is smooth, soft and a little shiny. Cover with plastic wrap and rest for at least 10 minutes.

Roll out your filo pastry sheets (see **Kneading and rolling filo pastry sheets, overleaf**), laying them on a work surface dusted with cornflour.

assembly

1 egg
2 heaped tablespoons Greek yoghurt
25g/¼ stick butter, melted
1 tablespoon nigella seeds

Preheat the oven to 200°C/400°F. In a small bowl, whisk together the egg and Greek yoghurt to make a glaze – set aside while you shape the pie. Brush half the melted butter over the inside of a 30cm/12" tart pan or baking dish.

Fill the rolled dough sheets – working one length of dough at a time, distribute some of the filling down the middle and fold the long edges over to make a long tube. Cut the tube in half (this will make it easier to lift) and coil each piece in the bottom of your tart pan, working from the outside in to make one even layer.

Drizzle the other half of the melted butter over the pie and brush over half the egg and yoghurt glaze. Bake for 20 minutes, then remove from the oven, brush with the rest of the glaze and sprinkle with the nigella seeds. Turn the pie and return to the oven, baking for a further 10-20 minutes, until evenly golden.

✶

Serve with enough for seconds. And thirds.

kneading the filo pastry dough

Cut off a slice of dough, as you would a loaf of bread. Shape 1 piece into a rough rectangle and feed through a pasta machine on setting 1, keeping everything dusted with cornflour. Fold the dough in half and run through the machine again, repeating this process about 10 times, to give the dough a final knead.

rolling the filo pastry sheets

Continue running the dough through the machine, keeping everything well dusted with cornflour, increasing the setting one stage at a time until the pastry is as thin as possible (setting 6-7). Lay the sheets on a work surface dusted with cornflour.

battered halloumi and chips
with lemon pickled onions and coriander peas

✱

Deep-fried halloumi in a seasoned chickpea crust – one of life's truly great things to put in your mouth. Crispy, deliciously flavourful batter with a meltingly tender halloumi centre. Served with spicy roasted potatoes, zingy pickled onions and herby peas.

serves 4-6

battered halloumi

2 packs halloumi, cut in 2cm/1" cubes
4 garlic cloves, crushed
2 teaspoons ground coriander
60g/²⁄₃ cup chickpea flour
40g/¹⁄₃ cup cornflour
1 teaspoon turmeric
1 teaspoon smoked hot paprika
2 teaspoons mustard seeds
½ teaspoon baking soda

Pat the halloumi dry with paper towels. Mix together the garlic, ground coriander and lots of pepper and rub this mixture on the halloumi. Set aside to season. Whisk together the rest of the ingredients with 1 teaspoon flaky salt and 120g/½ cup cold water – the batter should have the consistency of double cream.

Preheat the oven to 160°C/325°F to keep the halloumi warm as you cook it in batches. Cover a baking tray with 2 layers of kitchen towel to soak up excess oil. Heat the oil in a large pan to 170°C/350°F – if you don't have a thermometer, at this temperature a cube of bread will brown in 45-60 seconds.

Coat a piece of halloumi in the batter and drip off any excess. Slide carefully into the oil and repeat with 7-8 more pieces – any more and the pan will become too crowded and the oil temperature will drop. Fry for about 5 minutes, until crisp and lightly golden, turning occasionally in the oil so they cook evenly. Remove with a slotted spoon, drain on the baking tray and keep hot while you fry the rest of the cheese. Serve immediately.

spicy roasted potatoes

800g/4 large potatoes
2 flat tablespoons cornflour
½ teaspoon hot chilli powder
1 teaspoon coriander seeds, ground
1 teaspoon brown mustard seeds

Preheat the oven to 200°C/400°F. Cut the potatoes into fries (no need to peel) and toss with the spices and a good drizzle of oil. Use a non-stick baking tray or cover a baking tray with baking paper (don't use foil, it sticks!) and lay the potatoes in a single layer, without touching. Bake until browned and crispy and season with a sprinkle of flaky salt and a little pepper before serving.

lemon pickled onions

2 red onions, thinly sliced
1 lemon, juice only
1 hot red chilli, sliced thinly

Juice the lemon. Toss the onions and chilli with the juice and season with ½ teaspoon flaky salt and lots of pepper. Set aside to marinate for 1 hour.

coriander peas

1 teaspoon cumin seeds
1 onion, chopped fine
2 garlic cloves, crushed
250g/9oz shelled peas (frozen is fine)
3 hot green chillies, chopped fine
½ lemon, juice only
handful fresh coriander, leaves and stems, roughly chopped

Heat a medium pan over medium heat until hot. Add a knob of butter, then the cumin seeds and fry until fragrant. Add the chopped onion and garlic and cook until softened, about 10 minutes. Add the peas, chillies, ½ teaspoon flaky salt and 100g/7 tablespoons water. Cover and steam for a couple of minutes, until the peas are cooked through. Cook off any excess water if needed. Juice the lemon and stir through the peas with the fresh coriander.

to serve

250g/8oz Greek yoghurt
1 lemon, cut into wedges

✱

Serve the crispy halloumi just-out-of-the-oil, with Greek yoghurt to dip and fresh lemon for tangy tartness.

roasted aubergine & halloumi pizza
with crème fraîche and nigella seed crust

*

Crispy, nutty, thin-crust pizza with roasted aubergine purée, toasty halloumi, fresh mozzarella, blobs of crème fraîche and a crunchy nigella seed crust. Earthy, creamy, cheesy, caramelised goodness.

per 30cm/12" pizza

aubergine and halloumi pizza

1 ball **pizza dough (page 146)**
1 recipe **roasted aubergine purée (overleaf)**
½ pack halloumi, finely grated
½ ball fresh mozzarella
4 heaped tablespoons crème fraîche
1 tablespoon nigella seeds

Shape the pizza and arrange on a pizza peel (see **Stretching the pizza**, page 150).

Spread the aubergine purée over the base of the pizza, leaving the crust puffy and exposed. Pile the grated halloumi in little heaps around the pizza. Tear over the mozzarella and dollop on the crème fraîche.

Drizzle oil over the puffed pizza rim and sprinkle the crust with nigella seeds and a pinch of flaky salt.

See **Cooking the pizza**, page 151.

roasted aubergine purée

1 aubergine
squeeze of lemon juice
1 garlic clove, crushed

Poke the aubergine all over with a knife and roast in a hot oven for about 1 hour, until very soft all over – you can roast it while heating the oven for the pizza. Scrape the aubergine flesh out of the skin and blend with ¼ teaspoon flaky salt, a squeeze of lemon juice and the crushed garlic. Set aside until ready to cook the pizza.

to serve

few sprigs fresh thyme, leaves only

✱

Serve the pizza piping hot, with a few leaves of thyme sprinkled over.

spring greens & halloumi pizza
with fresh red chilli and oregano crust

✶

Crispy, nutty, thin-crust pizza baked with layers of shredded greens, salty halloumi, fresh mozzarella and fiery chilli. The crunchy, puffy edge is seasoned with herbs and flaky salt – great for dipping.

per 30cm/12" pizza

1 ball pizza dough (page 146)
¼ head spring greens
½ pack halloumi, cut into small cubes
½ ball fresh mozzarella
1 hot fresh chilli, thinly sliced
½ teaspoon dried oregano

Shape the pizza and arrange on a pizza peel (see **Stretching the pizza**, page 150).

Cut away any tough stems from the spring greens and slice into 2cm/1" shreds. Add to a bowl and toss with a splash of oil and ¼ teaspoon flaky salt.

Cover the base of the pizza with the greens, leaving the crust puffy and exposed. Scatter over the cubed halloumi, torn pieces of mozzarella and fresh chilli.

Drizzle oil around the puffed pizza rim and sprinkle the crust with oregano and a pinch of flaky salt.

See **Cooking the pizza**, page 151.

✶

Serve the pizza piping hot, with a few scattered herbs or flowers.

broccoli & halloumi pizza
with pickled chillies and sumac crust

✱

Crispy, nutty, thin-crust pizza with creamy broccoli-garlic purée, chunks of halloumi and fresh mozzarella, with pickled chillies and a crunchy sumac crust.

per 30cm/12" pizza

broccoli and halloumi pizza

1 ball <u>pizza dough (page 146)</u>
1 recipe <u>broccoli purée (overleaf)</u>
½ pack halloumi, cut into small cubes
½ ball fresh mozzarella
1 teaspoon sumac
1-2 hot pickled chillies, finely sliced
1 teaspoon pink peppercorns

Shape the pizza and arrange on a pizza peel (see **<u>Stretching the pizza</u>, page 150**).

Spread the broccoli purée over the base of the pizza, leaving the crust puffy and exposed. Scatter over the halloumi cubes and tear over the mozzarella.

Drizzle oil around the puffed pizza rim and sprinkle the crust with sumac and a pinch of flaky salt.

See **<u>Cooking the pizza</u>, page 151**.

broccoli-garlic purée

150g/½ head broccoli, cut into florets
1 garlic clove, crushed
100ml/7 tablespoons cold-pressed oil

Bring a pot of water to the boil and cook the broccoli until fairly soft.

Add to a food processor and blend with the garlic, oil and ½ teaspoon flaky salt to a very creamy purée. Set aside until you need to top the pizza.

✶

Serve the pizza piping hot, with the pickled chillies and pink peppercorns sprinkled over.

chewy, crunchy, nutty pizza dough
with a thin, crispy base and puffed, airy crust

*

I have dedicated much of my life to the pursuit of amazing pizza, that elusive delight. For something so simple, made of such few ingredients, the variety – and difference in quality – is staggering. I have eaten pizza all over the world, trained with master Roman pizza maker Gabriele Bonci and even run my own pizzeria. I have made pizza in every home oven I have ever had (and with my travel-happy life, that's a lot of ovens), each with its own quirks, for good and for bad. This recipe is the result of that labour – the best of all pizza worlds.

makes 6 x 30cm/12" pizzas

making the dough

1 level teaspoon dry yeast or 16g/½oz fresh yeast
370g/3 cups strong white bread flour
370g/2 ¾ cups strong whole wheat bread flour
2 teaspoons honey
1 level teaspoon vital wheat gluten

Add the yeast and 600g/2 ½ cups lukewarm water (any hotter will kill the yeast) to a mixer – stand mixers and food processors both work well. Whizz for a few seconds to dissolve the yeast. Add all the other ingredients and mix until fully combined – don't knead yet. Rest for 5 minutes to allow the flour to hydrate.

Add 2 teaspoons flaky salt and knead for a further 8 minutes. Check the dough isn't too wet – the dough should be very sticky, but should have pulled away from the sides of the mixer. If it hasn't, add a little more flour and mix again for a minute or so. If it doesn't seem sticky at all, add a little water – this needs to be a high hydration dough to survive the long cook in a domestic oven.

semolina, for dusting

Drizzle the inside of a large bowl with a little oil (the dough will double in size). Scrape the sticky dough onto a work surface dusted with semolina and imagining the dough has four corners, fold each corner of the dough into the centre – this is easiest with a dough/bench scraper.

Turn the dough over so the folded edges face down and place in the bowl. Cover with plastic wrap and leave to rise in a warm place for 45 minutes.

Turn the bowl over onto a surface dusted with semolina and let the dough drop out. Again fold each corner of the dough into the centre, turn over so the folded edges face down and place back in the bowl. This folding technique adds bigger air bubbles to your dough and makes the crumb lighter. Cover again with plastic wrap and leave for a further 45 minutes.

Turn the dough out again onto a dusted work surface and slice into 6 equal pieces with a serrated knife or scraper.

See **Shaping and rising the dough balls**, <u>overleaf</u>.

shaping the dough balls

Form each piece of dough into a tight ball by tucking the bottom edges under, all the way round, deflating the dough as you shape — you are stretching a gluten cloak around the dough ball.

Rest the balls on a floured work surface, drizzle with a little oil and cover loosely with clingfilm.

rising the dough balls

Rise the shaped dough balls for 1 hour, until very airy and puffed, then gently transfer to a large work surface dusted with semolina.

Turn on the oven after you shape the dough balls and it will heat as they rise (see **Cooking the pizza**, overleaf).

stretching the pizza

When the dough is ready, place 1 ball on a well dusted work surface.

Using your fingers, gently press the dough into a medium round, working from the centre outward and leaving a 2cm/1" ring around the edge of the dough that is not deflated – it is this airy rim that will puff up beautifully in the oven.

Gently stretch the pizza into a large round. Take care not to break the gluten strands and make a hole – this dough is delicate. Try to feel the stretchy gluten in the dough and don't pull it more than it can handle.

If your dough is very tight, a 5 minute rest between stretches can help. You're trying to get the dough as thin as possible, while still leaving some air for lightness and texture – put that rolling pin down!

cooking the pizza

semolina, for dusting
baking stone or steel

When you finish shaping the dough balls, start heating the oven to maximum temperature. Getting your oven as hot as possible is important for great home pizza. This means you can only bake 1 pizza at a time, otherwise the temperature drops too much and the pizza bakes dry and tough.

A baking stone is essential – you can use your heaviest baking tray if you don't have a stone, but the pizza will bake much slower and drier. Put your stone (or tray) in the oven, about 8cm/3" from the top and heat for 1 hour (while the dough balls are rising). Your oven and stone should now be smoking hot!

Arrange the pizza on a peel (a flat board for moving pizza in and out of the oven) – if you don't have a pizza peel, a large piece of cardboard is the best substitute. Add the toppings. Give the peel a little shake to make sure the pizza hasn't stuck anywhere underneath – poke a little semolina under there if it has, but try to avoid this.

Working quickly but carefully, remove the pizza stone from the oven, put it on something heatproof and quickly close the oven door to keep in the heat. Gently shake the pizza from the peel and onto the stone, starting by resting the tip of the peel on the far edge of the stone.

When the pizza is on the stone, quickly rearrange the dough into a thin, even round using your fingers (careful!) – you have about 30 seconds to do this before the pizza starts to set on the hot stone. Put the pizza and stone in the oven and bake until everything looks golden and bubbly, about 10 minutes – do not undercook.

Remove the pizza and stone from the oven and transfer the pizza to a serving platter using the peel. If you are baking more pizzas (of course you are!), scrape off any excess semolina and return the stone to the oven to heat while you and your diners eat.

✳

Serve the crispy pizza topped with all kinds of wonderful cheeses, vegetables and herbs.

halloumi & spinach tamales
with guacamole, chipotle cream and salad

✶

Tamales are made from a rich corn dough, whipped until fluffy, then steamed until lightly set – they are incredibly moist and creamy. Here stuffed with strands of halloumi, wilted spinach and roasted peanuts and served with a herby coriander salad, guacamole and smoky chipotle crème fraîche. Enlist help with wrapping the tamales and make enough for leftovers.

serves 6-8

halloumi, spinach and peanut filling

600g/1lb 5oz fresh spinach
1 pack halloumi, finely grated
100g/⅔ cups peanuts, toasted and roughly ground

Bring a large pot of water to the boil with 1 tablespoon coarse sea salt. Add the spinach (do this in 2 batches) and cook until just wilted, about 1 minute. Drain and rinse to cool.

Pile about half the spinach into a clean tea towel and twist to squeeze out as much water as possible. Roughly chop and add to a large bowl. Stir through the grated halloumi, ground peanuts, ½ teaspoon flaky salt and a few screws of pepper.

guacamole

1 lime, juice only
1 garlic clove, crushed
2 ripe avocados
handful fresh coriander, leaves and stems, chopped

Juice the lime, add the garlic to the lime juice and set aside for 20 minutes – this effectively cooks the garlic. When the garlic is ready, peel and dice the avocado and add to a small bowl. Stir through the coriander, garlic, half the lime juice and ½ teaspoon flaky salt. Taste and adjust the seasoning if necessary with more salt and lime juice.

tamale dough

350g/3 cups masa harina (or finely ground polenta)
250g/2 ¼ sticks butter, softened
2 teaspoons baking powder

Mix the masa or polenta with 500g/2 cups water and set aside for 15 minutes to rehydrate.

In a food processor or stand mixer, beat the butter, baking powder and 2 teaspoons flaky salt until well whipped.

Add about a third of the rehydrated masa, breaking up any big pieces and beat with the butter until thoroughly incorporated. Repeat with the rest of the masa, scraping down as needed. Drizzle in 250ml/1 cup + 3 tablespoons water and continue beating the buttery dough until it is lightened and very creamy. Cover and refrigerate for 1 hour.

Cut 30 pieces of baking paper (20 x 15cm/8 x 6"). Remove the dough from the fridge and rewhip to loosen, adding a little extra water if needed.

See **Wrapping the tamales**.

Add them to a steamer, wrap the top tightly with foil and steam on high for 1 hour. Remove from the heat, uncover (careful!) and rest for 10 minutes to firm up.

wrapping the tamales

Smear a small rectangle (10 x 6cm/4 x 3") on one of the pieces of baking paper and layer over 1-2 tablespoons filling.

Roll the tamale dough over the filling and form the package into a tube, folding one end over to hold in the dough. Sit the tamales upright in a steamer – tip the steamer on its side at the beginning so the first tamales lay flat, then turn it the right way when it starts to fill.

coriander pesto salad

big handful fresh coriander, leaves and stems
1 garlic clove, crushed
½ lime, juice only
100ml/7 tablespoons cold-pressed oil
1 head romaine lettuce, sliced in 2cm/1" strips

Add all the ingredients to a food processor with ¼ teaspoon flaky salt and blend to a smooth pesto. Check the seasoning and set aside until you are ready to serve the salad.

Just before serving, toss the salad leaves with the pesto so everything is evenly coated.

chipotle cream

250ml/8oz crème fraîche
2 chipotles in adobo or 2 tablespoons chipotle paste

Blend or crush the chipotles into a paste if necessary. Stir the chilli and any spicy juices through the crème fraîche to mostly combine.

✱

Unwrap the steamy packages at the table and serve the buttery tamales with zingy coriander salad, guacamole and little dollops of chipotle cream.

squash & halloumi Wellington

with winter vegetables, Yorkshire pudding and roasted garlic sauce

*

Make the vegetarian option the star of the Christmas table with this beautiful Wellington. Sweet butternut squash and salty halloumi layers wrapped in puff pastry, with a little cream to keep everything moist. Served with caramelised potatoes, parsnips, mushrooms and red onion, huge Yorkshire puddings and a creamy, roasted garlic sauce.

serves 4-6

squash and halloumi Wellington

250g/9oz all-butter puff pastry
2 packs halloumi, thinly sliced
½ butternut squash, thinly sliced
100ml/7 tablespoons double cream
⅛ whole nutmeg, freshly grated
½ egg
50ml/¼ cup milk

Preheat the oven to 200°C/400°F. Roll the pastry very thinly into a 40 x 50cm/15 x 20" rectangle and lay on a large piece of baking paper (to help shape the Wellington).

Building in an oblong shape, layer pumpkin, halloumi, nutmeg, a pinch of flaky salt and 1 tablespoon cream in multiple layers, finishing with a layer of pumpkin.

Fold one long side of the pastry over the pumpkin layers, then the other long side to overlap in a seal. Tuck in the short edges, as you would when wrapping a present, trimming off any excess so the pastry is relatively even all the way round. Turn the whole package over carefully (use the paper to help you) and lay on a baking tray.

Beat the egg and milk together and glaze the Wellington all over. Bake for 40-50 minutes, until the inside is tender to the point of a knife. Rest for 15 minutes before slicing and serving.

roasted winter vegetables

800g/1lb 12oz baby potatoes, halved
2 parsnips, cut into strips
250g/9oz chestnut mushrooms, halved
1 red onion, cut into 2cm/1" pieces
1 tablespoon Dijon mustard
handful fresh rosemary or thyme, leaves only, chopped

Preheat the oven to 200°C/400°F (or roast with the Wellington) and heat a baking tray. Toss the potatoes in a little oil and add to the hot tray (skin side down at first), roasting for 20 minutes. Add the parsnips and bake them together with the potatoes for a further 20 minutes.

While the parsnips are cooking, spread the mushrooms over a separate baking tray, drizzle over a little oil and roast for 10 minutes. Add the onion to the mushrooms and roast together for a further 10 minutes.

Scrape everything into a serving dish and toss the roasted vegetables with the mustard, herbs and ½ teaspoon flaky salt. Return to the oven for a further 5 minutes to roast with the seasonings before serving.

creamy roasted garlic sauce

1 head garlic
240ml/1 cup double cream
1 heaped teaspoon Dijon mustard

Preheat the oven to 200°C/400°F (or roast with the Wellington). Slice the top 1cm/½" off the garlic, wrap in a twist of baking paper or foil and bake for 40 minutes, until lightly browned and well softened. Pop out the cloves and blend the roasted garlic with the cream and mustard. Heat gently in small saucepan to serve.

Yorkshire pudding

3 large eggs
150g/⅔ cup whole milk
130g/1 cup plain flour

Blend all ingredients with ½ teaspoon flaky salt and rest for as long as possible – resting in the fridge overnight radically improves the flavour, texture and rise of Yorkshire puddings.

When you are ready to cook, preheat the oven to 220°C/425°F (or raise the oven for the final 30 minutes of cooking the vegetables) and arrange an oven shelf near the top. Add your Yorkshire pudding containers, each with a little drizzle of oil.

After about 10 minutes, carefully remove and distribute the batter between the hot containers, filling them about three-quarters full. Bake until very well risen and crispy, 15-20 minutes – don't open the oven until they have finished rising and have cooked for a further few minutes to set.

*

Serve with a roaring fire.

substitutions

salt

I use **flaky sea salt** for everything except seasoning big pans of water (for that I use **coarse sea salt**). Flaky salt is natural, it retains sea water minerals, crumbles easily in your fingers and looks beautiful sprinkled over food. Flaky salt has twice the volume of fine table salt, so if substituting use half:
1 teaspoon flaky salt = ½ teaspoon table salt

Truffle salt is lovely on eggs and is a very cost-effective way to get a little truffle aroma in your food – but any salt will be fine.

flavourings

Don't have any **chipotle in adobo**, **harissa** or **mustard**? Use chilli powder, chilli sauce, miso paste, even Marmite, for similarly concentrated, savoury flavours.
Nutritional yeast (pictured right) is an easy, healthy way to give vegetarian food a massive umami boost, but if you don't have a health food shop nearby, just leave it out.
Dried tomatoes are fruity and savoury – dried mushrooms, fresh herbs, caramelised onions and garlic are good substitutes. **Sumac**, **pomegranate molasses**, **barberries**, **lemon** and **vinegars** have similarly tart flavours, so can easily be swapped with each other. If you don't have a particular **fruit**, **vegetable**, **herb**, **spice** or **seed**, just use what you have or leave it out.

oils

Cold-pressed oils – oils that have been made in a way which best preserves their nutritional content – are my favourite for everyday use, especially uncooked in salad dressings and dips. I mostly use **rapeseed oil**, olive oil, **butter** and coconut oil, but they are all just fats and can be swapped with any other oil with minimal taste issues. For deep frying, any cheap, refined vegetable oil is fine – peanut oil is better, but expensive.

flours, grains & bread

Flours can be a little more complicated to substitute as they are often what controls structure in a recipe, but there is still a lot of flexibility. If you don't have **spelt or atta flour**, use any other whole wheat flour, or failing that, any white flour. **Chickpea flour** is made from protein-rich pulses, and not grains – if being used as a binder, any other flour can be used. If making a batter, plain white flour is the best substitute. If you can't find **masa harina**, finely ground cornmeal or polenta works well.

Freekeh and **brown basmati rice** can be changed for any whole or white grain, but the water amounts and timings will need to be adjusted – check your packet or online.

I have included **sourdough bread** throughout the book, some made by Leeds Bread Co-op, some home-baked. If you have access to real bread where you live, I strongly encourage you to seek it out – it's radically healthier than factory bread and, most importantly, is tastes much, much better. But as ever, use what you have.

equipment

I use a **food processor** because it helps me make my own breads, cakes, pastries, pastas and pestos for every single meal. But you don't need expensive equipment to make amazing food. Every recipe in this book was made with my cheapest food processor – it cost me £10 from a charity shop and dates from the 1980s. So if you're on a budget, there are plenty of options, though you will definitely get a better piece of equipment – one that can handle daily use and knead strong doughs – if you buy secondhand. Unfortunately, there's not much to recommend new, low-end machines, so bear that in mind when choosing.

Having said that, anything you can do with a **food processor**, you do by hand – the only real difference is hard labour, but by all means knead or crush by hand if they are the tools you have available. A **stand mixer** is great for doughs and an **immersion blender** works well for sauces, dressings and mayonnaise. If kneading doughs by hand or using a stand mixer, knead 4-5 times longer than a food processor, stopping when the dough looks as described in the recipe.

index & glossary

freekeh
Roasted, cracked green wheat, often used in Middle Eastern cuisines. A nutty, chewy, healthy whole grain, rich in proteins, vitamins and minerals.

G

garam masala
An incredibly fragrant mix of ground coriander, ginger, cinnamon, cumin, black pepper, allspice, cardamom, clove, bay, cassia and nutmeg. Stirred into south Asian dishes towards the end of cooking.

Gruyère
A hard, raw milk cheese made in the Swiss mountains. Nutty and sweet when young, it becomes earthy and complex as it matures and melts beautifully.

H

harissa
An oily, spicy, North African chilli paste, rich with roasted peppers, chillies, rose and other delicious seasonings.

halloumi cannelloni 98-101
halloumi choux pastry fritters 116-119
halloumi onion bhaji waffles 54-57
halloumi, spinach and peanut tamales 152-157
halloumi, watermelon and basil salad 32-35
harissa halloumi kebabs 90-93
harissa halloumi salad 50-53
marinated halloumi in vine leaves 102-105
palak halloumi 78-81
potato, pumpkin and halloumi gratin 86-89
rich, spicy tomato curry 66-69
roasted aubergine and halloumi pizza 136-139
roasted halloumi, cherry tomatoes and garlic 84
roasted winter vegetables 160
spelt za'atar crackers 122
spinach and halloumi pie 124-129
tomato risotto 82-85
whole wheat halloumi parathas 22-25

honey
avocado and watercress salad 96
crispy halloumi chipotle burgers 94-97
moist, creamy cornbread 26-27

L

leek
harissa halloumi kebabs 90-93

lemon
basil pesto 76
battered halloumi and chips 130-136
caramelised halloumi potato wedges 28-31
coriander peas 134
courgette and halloumi burgers 74-77
garlic, lemon and herb butter 24
garlic mayonnaise 114
halloumi cannelloni 98-101
halloumi fries 112-115
halloumi onion bhaji waffles 54-57
halloumi, watermelon and basil salad 32-35
harissa halloumi kebabs 90-93
harissa halloumi salad 50-53
lemon asparagus 76
lemon pickled onions 132
marinated halloumi in vine leaves 102-105
palak halloumi 78-81
spinach and halloumi pie 124-129
sumac yoghurt 30
tomato-avocado salad 104
tomato pesto 52
whole wheat halloumi parathas 22-25

lettuce
coriander pesto salad 156
courgette and halloumi burgers 74-77
crispy halloumi chipotle burgers 94-97
halloumi, spinach and peanut tamales 152-157
halloumi, watermelon and basil salad 32-35
harissa halloumi kebabs 90-93
harissa halloumi salad 50-53
potato, pumpkin and halloumi gratin 86-89
romaine salad with cider vinaigrette 88

lime
coriander pesto salad 156
guacamole 153

M

masa harina, see **corn**

masa harina
Soaked, cooked corn kernels ground into flour.
Used in Mexican and central American cuisines to
make breads and doughs like tortillas and tamales.

milk
Yorkshire pudding 161

mint
courgette and halloumi burgers 74-77
halloumi, watermelon and basil salad 32-35
harissa halloumi salad 50-53

mozzarella
broccoli and halloumi pizza 142-145
roasted aubergine and halloumi pizza 136-139
spring greens and halloumi pizza 140-141

mushroom
full English breakfast 38-41
halloumi bacon and mushroom sandwich 42-43
harissa halloumi kebabs 90-93
rich, spicy tomato curry 66-69
roasted winter vegetables 160

mustard
cheese toastie 58-59
creamy roasted garlic sauce 160
crispy halloumi chipotle burgers 94-97
halloumi bacon and mushroom sandwich 42-43
halloumi choux pastry fritters 116-119
romaine salad with cider vinaigrette 88

mustard, seed
battered halloumi and chips 130-136

I work with all things food.

Cheese is one of my life's great passions and
I can regularly be found writing on the topic.

I truly cannot thank you enough for your
support. Get in touch or just get more
vegetarian, cheesy inspiration –

Delicious
from scratch

fine vegetarian recipes

www.deliciousfromscratch.com

CPSIA information can be obtained
at www.ICGtesting.com
Printed in the USA
BVHW02*0903120918
527279BV00014B/78/P